A Run to the Bay

Written by Sandra Iversen

Clay and I are going for a run today.
I cannot see,
so I don't know the way.
Clay has a rope.
I hold the rope.

rope

We are going to run down to the bay.
It is a good day for a run.
Clay and I set off down the street.

We pass the park.
I can hear children playing.
I can hear skateboards
going up and down on the ramp.
We run on down to the bay.

skateboard ramp

We get to the bay.
I like it here.
I like to feel the sand on my feet.
I like to hear the waves.
When it is windy,
I can feel the spray on my face.

sand

I hold the rope and we run home.
This time we cross the main street.
I hear the cars,
but I am safe with Clay.

main street

11

We are home.

"Thank you, Clay," I say.